RASIS

Discaces

Susie Brooks

Published in paperback in 2016 by Wayland
Copyright © Wayland 2016

Editor: Elizabeth Brent

Designer: Rocket Design (East Anglia) Ltd

Dewey number: 910.9'152-dc23

ISBN          978 0 7502 9072 2
eBook ISBN    978 0 7502 9071 5

Printed in China

10 9 8 7 6 5 4 3 2 1

Picture acknowledgements:
The author and publisher would like to thank the following
for allowing their pictures to be reproduced in this publication:
Pictures by Shutterstock except for p4–5: Stefan Chabluk; p6:
DeAgostini/Getty Images; p7: Stefan Chabluk (bottom left); p8:
Paul Harris/JAI/Corbis; p10: Frans Lanting/Corbis; p11: Thomas
Marent,/Visuals Unlimited/Corbis (bottom left),  Wolfgang Kaehler
/LightRocket via Getty Images (bottom right); p12: Scubazoo
/SuperStock/Corbis (left), Stefan Chabluk (right); p15: Michael &
Patricia Fogden/CORBIS; p17: Nick Fox/Shutterstock.com (top left);
p18: Scott Wallace/Getty Images (bottom left), Monica Dalmasso/
Design Pics/Corbis (bottom middle); p19: Carlos Garcia Rawlins/
Reuters/Corbis (top right), David Hiser/National Geographic Creative
/Corbis (middle), Pal Teravagimov/Shutterstock.com (bottom left),
DeAgostini/Getty Images (bottom right); p20: Scott Wallace/Getty
Images (top left), PASCAL PAVANI/AFP/Getty Images (bottom left);
p23: Cyril Ruoso/ JH Editorial/Minden Pictures/Corbis (bottom);
p25: W. Perry Conway/CORBIS (top); Pete Oxford/Getty Images (top right),
Alex Wild/Visuals Unlimited/Corbis (bottom right); p27 Wayne Lynch/All
Canada Photos/Corbis (top left); p28: Rich Carey/Shutterstock.com (bottom)
 p29: Stefan Chabluk (top and bottom) Disclaimer: Every effort has been
made to trace the copyright holder but if you feel you have the rights to
any images contained in this book then please contact the publisher.
The website addresses (URLs) included in this book were valid at
the time of going to press. However, it is possible that contents or
addresses may have changed since the publication of this book. No
responsibility for any such changes can be accepted by either the
author or the Publisher.

Wayland, an imprint of Hachette Children's Group
Part of Hodder & Stoughton
Carmelite House
50 Victoria Embankment
London
EC4Y 0DZ

An Hachette UK Company
www.hachette.co.uk
www.hachettechildrens.co.uk

# CONTENTS

# Where on Earth are rainforests?

YOU MIGHT ONLY NEED A FEW HOURS IN A RAINFOREST TO FIND A BUG UNKNOWN TO SCIENCE.

Picture a belt around the middle of the globe. That's where you'll find most rainforests. Tropical rainforests grow close to the Equator where it's hot and – the clue is in the name – rainy! There are also some temperate rainforests, which grow in cooler (but still very wet) parts of the world.

Rainforests grow on every continent except Antarctica, and they benefit all of our lives. In this book you'll discover WHERE, HOW and WHY ON EARTH rainforests are so important!

### BIG DADDY
The Amazon is by far the biggest rainforest. Most of it lies in Brazil.

### ANTS
You can find about 50 types of ant on a single tree in Peru – as many as there are in the whole of the UK!

 Cloud forest (see p12)

 Temperate rainforest (see p16)

 Tropical rainforest

## WARM AND WET

Tropical rainforests:

- Lie between the Tropic of Cancer and the Tropic of Capricorn
- Are consistently warm (temperatures average around 25°C)
- Have regular rainfall through the year (totalling 2,000-10,000 mm).

## 2,000 MM OF RAINFALL MEANS...

A single square metre of rainforest gets 2,000 litres of rainfall every year - that's an average of 5.5 litres each day. Times it by the whole Amazon rainforest, and you get over 30 TRILLION litres falling daily (enough to fill 12 million Olympic pools!).

### BOUNTIFUL BUGS

Tropical rainforests are a creepy crawly paradise, home to 80% of all insects.

### FAMILY

One of our closest relatives – a chimp called the bonobo – lives in the Congo rainforest.

### STRIPY

The okapi of the Ituri rainforest looks like a zebra but is related to the giraffe!

### DINO FOREST

Taman Negara (Malaysia) is one of the world's oldest rainforests. It's been around for 130 million years – so dinosaurs probably walked in it!

TROPICAL RAINFORESTS COVER LESS THAN 2% OF THE EARTH'S SURFACE, BUT CONTAIN OVER HALF OF ALL SPECIES!

# Why does it rain so much?

It's all to do with where rainforests are on Earth. Around the Equator, there's more direct sunlight hitting the land and sea than anywhere else on the planet. The heat makes water evaporate into the air, where it rises, cools, forms clouds and… falls again as rain.

LARGE RAINFORESTS CREATE AS MUCH AS 50–80 PER CENT OF THEIR OWN RAIN.

SOME OF THE WORLD'S BIGGEST RIVERS FLOW THROUGH RAINFORESTS – NO PRIZES FOR GUESSING WHY!

Rainforests make a lot of rain themselves! Some rainwater collects on the treetops, then evaporates to form more clouds. In addition, plants give off their own water vapour. A big rainforest tree can 'sweat' hundreds of litres of moisture in a day – this process is called transpiration.

In a typical tropical rainforest, 60 mm of rain can fall in an hour. That's like tipping six bucket-loads of water onto a single square metre! When it's not raining, the air feels damp and 'sticky' because of the high humidity. Around 80 per cent of the air in a rainforest is made up of water vapour.

Rain falling on a rainforest can take as long as 10 minutes to reach the ground! Why? It has to travel through all these layers:

## CANOPY LAYERS

25221. Neg 34455

### EMERGENTS
These lanky trees can be 60 metres tall. They poke out above the rest of the forest, where there's no escaping the Sun, rain and wind.

### CANOPY
Most trees in the forest stop at this level (about 30 metres above the ground), forming a thick, leafy 'umbrella' that shades everything beneath.

### UNDERSTOREY
In this dim, humid layer, plants grow large leaves to soak up what light they can.

### FOREST FLOOR
Only about 2% of sunlight actually gets this far. It's dark and damp, with lots of rotting leaves and fungi among the tree roots and trunks.

## CLIMATE CONTROL
Moisture from rainforests travels around the world. Scientists have found that forests in the Congo, in Africa, affect rainfall in America's Midwest! Rainforests also affect the global climate by taking in carbon dioxide and giving off oxygen. Plants do this in a process called photosynthesis.

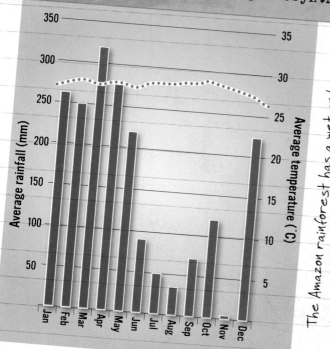

The Amazon rainforest has a wet and a drier season, as you can see from this climate chart for Manaus, Brazil.

Most rainforest animals live in the canopy layer - including colugos like this one. Monkeys, frogs, lizards, snakes, sloths and even small wildcats also make their home here.

# Which rainforest has the most trees?

## THE AMAZON HAS ABOUT 55 TREES FOR EVERY PERSON ON THE PLANET!

The Amazon wins, hands down. Although numbers are changing all the time (and no one's really going to count!), scientists think there may be 390 billion trees in this vast South American forest. That's more than all the stars in the Milky Way!

The Amazon is the world's biggest rainforest. Measuring about 5.5 million square kilometres, it's more than ten times the size of Spain. Most of the forest falls in Brazil, followed by Peru and Colombia. There are smaller parts in Venezuela, Ecuador, Bolivia, Guyana, Suriname and French Guiana.

A lot of the water that falls in this region drains into the mighty Amazon river. During extra rainy times of year, the river floods and leaves huge stretches of forest underwater. These flooded forests, known as igapo or varzea, have adapted to cope with the seasonal soaking.

## A FIFTH OF THE WORLD'S RIVER WATER FLOWS THROUGH THE AMAZON!

## NATURE NUMBERS

The Amazon is home to about:

3,000 types of fish

430 mammal species

40,000 plant species (including 16,000 types of tree)

1,300 bird species

and a whopping 2.5 MILLION different types of insect.

If your beak's as long as a toucan's, you don't need to move far to reach for food!

The toucan is one of the noisiest jungle birds, with a range of calls from yelps to croaky squawks.

## LOST

In 1925, British explorer Percy Fawcett set off with his son and a friend to find the Lost City of Z, a mythical lost city in the Amazon. They all disappeared without a trace.

**BLOODSUCKER**

The giant Amazonian leech can grow to 45cm long and suck four times its bodyweight in blood!

LEECHES

# Why would a plant strangle a tree trunk?

With so many plants in a very tight space, competition is fierce in a rainforest. Plants have to fight for the sunlight and soil – even if it means strangling a tree to survive!

Some plants, known as epiphytes, make their homes on other plants. They grow mainly on the trunks, branches and even the leaves of trees. The strangler fig is an epiphyte. Instead of starting life underground, it seeds itself on a tree's branches. Here's how…

The original tree has completely gone!

**1** Birds or monkeys drop the seed high in a tree.

**2** The seedling fig sends long roots down to the ground.

**3** These roots grow quickly, wrapping round the tree and stealing its light and food from the soil.

**4** Eventually the tree dies and rots, leaving a huge, hollow strangler in its place. Creepy.

SOUTH AMERICANS CALL THE STRANGLER FIG MATAPALO, MEANING 'TREE KILLER'.

## SLOWCOACH!

The sloth is the slowest animal in the rainforest – so slow that plants called algae grow on its fur! The algae get water and shelter from the sloth. The sloth gets a nice green camouflage.

• A sloth may also be home to fungi, moths, beetles, cockroaches and other bugs. Biologists have found hundreds of insects living on a single sloth!

• Sloths sleep a LOT – about 15-20 hours a day.

• Try taking a whole minute to walk 2 metres. That's the speed of a sloth.

The best nutrients are in the surface soil, so instead of having deep roots – some big trees send out buttresses. These grow from the base of the trunk and can be over 5 metres tall!

## DECOMPOSERS

Fungi, and small creatures known as decomposers, feed on all the dead stuff on the rainforest floor. This breaks down nutrients from the plants and animals and releases them back into the soil. Next time you're in a rainforest, watch your step – the fungi can nibble feet too!

RAINFOREST CLINGERS

Lianas begin on the forest floor, but climb up towards the light by twisting round trees or attaching themselves with suckers.

Bromeliads grow on tree branches. They use their waxy leaves like a bowl to collect water – and water-loving creatures!

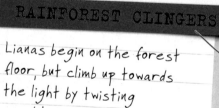

Fungi aren't plants, in fact, they're thought to be more like animals!

# Where are there forests in the clouds?

They're not actually floating in the sky – cloud forests grow on the slopes of mountains in tropical regions. They get their name because they're almost always cloaked in a layer of misty low cloud, sometimes right down to the ground.

## CLOUD-CATCHERS

Leaves capture water straight from the clouds, which are blown in among the trees by the wind.

## FORMING FOREST CLOUDS

Prevailing wind

Cloud forest

Mountain

CLOUD FORESTS CAN EXPERIENCE UP TO 10,000 MM OF RAIN A YEAR!

Cloud forests are rare, making up only about 0.2% of Earth's land surface. They tend to grow between 1,000 metres and 3,500 metres above sea level. It's cooler here than in a tropical rainforest, and everything is constantly dripping wet from the soggy air.

The trees in these high-altitude forests are shorter than lower down, often with gnarled trunks and branches. It's the perfect environment for damp-loving ferns, orchids, lichens and mosses – many trees look bright green all over from the moss growing on their bark!

## WILD FOODS

Wild relatives of many of our foods grow in cloud forests - including tomatoes, cucumbers, avocados, peppers and potatoes!

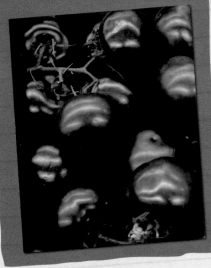

### FANCY FEATHERS

During the mating season, male quetzals grow resplendent tail feathers up to a metre long to impress the ladies.

In places like Costa Rica, ecotourism is a big source of income and helps to protect cloud forests. Many reserves have treetop walkways, ziplines and other adventures to enjoy.

## HOWLERS!

Listen out for howler monkeys, the loudest creatures on land. Even through thick jungle you can hear their call 5 km away.

At up to 130db, a howling howler monkey can be louder than a lawnmower or a low-flying jet!

# Why might a rainforest need elephants?

The Congo in Africa is the world's second-largest rainforest. It spans more than 3 million square kilometres. As with any rainforest, the trees here rely on wildlife to spread their seeds. And forest elephants are some of the best seed spreaders around...

African forest elephants live deep in the jungle and are smaller than their grassland relatives. Many types of seed won't germinate without passing through the elephants' digestive system. A 'dung study' – yes, that means inspecting poo! – found that the elephants eat more than 96 types of seed and can carry them as far as 57 km from their parent tree.

When plants and animals interact with each other, it's called an ecosystem. Within an ecosystem, all sorts of species depend on each other to survive.

# NUTTY NOTES!

The towering brazil nut tree grows only in South American rainforests. It survives thanks to a rodent called the agouti.

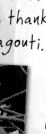

Brazil nuts grow inside a rock-hard casing, about the size of a grapefruit.

Agoutis are the only animal whose teeth can crack the casing to reach the nuts inside! They eat some of the nuts, and bury others. These can later grow into new trees.

When the brazil's seed-case is ripe, it falls from the tree at speeds of over 80 km/hr. Look out below!

## BEE'S TREES

Brazils also rely on other rainforest dwellers to exist...

Once a year, big flowers bloom on the brazil nut tree's branches.

Only the female orchid bee is strong enough to open and pollinate them.

So without orchids, brazil nut trees would not be pollinated.

Female orchid bees need a mate. The males attract females using a scent they get from an orchid.

## ANT RESCUE

Certain ants and caterpillars look after each other too. The caterpillar produces sweet-tasting chemicals on its back for the ants to eat. In return, the ants act as bodyguards and will even carry the caterpillar to safety if it is attacked!

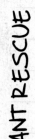

Imagine 60 grown-ups standing on each other's shoulders. They'd still struggle to reach the top of Hyperion, the tallest living tree! Towering at more than 115 metres, this giant coast redwood grows in the temperate rainforest of California, USA.

Temperate rainforests used to be found on almost every continent, but today only half (about 300,000 square kilometres) remain worldwide. The largest temperate rainforests are found on North America's Pacific Coast and stretch from northern California up into Canada.

| Tropical rainforests | Temperate rainforests |
| --- | --- |
| Hot temperatures year-round | Mild temperatures (cool to warm) |
| No major season changes | Long wet winter; short foggy summer |
| Mostly broad-leaved trees | Mostly conifers with needle-like leaves |
| Emergent trees above the canopy | No emergent trees |
| Most animals live in the canopy | Most animals live on or near the forest floor |

CHANDELIER
TREE

You can actually drive through
a coast redwood tree!

## Lean on me

When a tree dies and
falls in a temperate
rainforest, small seedlings
often take root on the
trunk. It becomes a
nurse log, covered in
mosses, ferns, lichens, and
eventually a whole
row of trees.

Hyperion makes
the Statue of
Liberty look
small!

115.61 m

93 m

The Roosevelt elk has
impressive antlers.
They protect it
against the bears and
cougars that hunt in US
temperate rainforests.

SCIENTISTS BELIEVE THAT
120-130 METRES IS THE MAXIMUM
POSSIBLE HEIGHT FOR A TREE.
HYPERION COMES CLOSE!

# Who builds houses in a rainforest?

Nature supplies the building materials!

A hot, steamy jungle, crawling with spiders and snakes... Would you want to live there? Millions of people do! Rainforests have been home to indigenous tribes for many hundreds of years, though in recent times their traditional lifestyle has come under threat.

In 1500, there were an estimated 6 million tribal people living in the Amazon. Today only about 250,000 remain. They include more than 200 ethnic groups, speaking around 170 different languages! There may still be about 50 tribes that have never had contact with the outside world.

ROUNDHOUSE

In a Yanomami village, everyone lives in one big, circular house made from logs and thatch.

TREEHOUSE

The Korowai of New Guinea build their homes on stilts or high up in the treetops.

MANY TRIBES PAINT THEIR FACES AND BODIES TO LOOK DECORATIVE, CAMOUFLAGED OR SCARY.

Rainforest people depend on the forest for their food and shelter. They hunt, fish and have learnt how to use thousands of plants for cooking, medicine and building. But they also know that respecting the rainforest is vital for their survival, so they never kill or chop down too much.

The Yanomami are handy with a bow and arrow.

## JUNGLE LIFE

## → HUNTERS

Like many indigenous tribes, the Penan of Borneo are hunter gatherers. They shoot their prey with blowpipes and poison darts.

## MILLIONS OF INDIGENOUS PEOPLE DIED FROM DISEASES SUCH AS MEASLES, BROUGHT BY EUROPEANS.

There are even modern cities in rainforests. You can't reach Iquitos in Peru by road!

## PYGMIES

The people of Africa's Congo rainforest are often described as pygmies because they're unusually short in height. Many are nomadic, moving camp several times a year.

* They put up temporary houses made from bent branches and leaves.

* The Mbuti will climb more than 30 metres into the canopy to collect honey from forest bees.

# How can a tree cure disease?

Amazingly, over a quarter of the medicines we use today have their origins in tropical rainforests – even though less than 1 per cent of rainforest plants have been tested for medical use! Imagine the potential for the rest.

A shaman is the ultimate plant pro.

Rainforests are like a natural chemist's. For thousands of years, indigenous people have been discovering uses for the chemicals found in plants. Today we all benefit as they find their way into modern medicine. Whatever is wrong with you, the chances are a jungle plant can help!

Scientists from around the world carry out important research in rainforests. The US National Cancer Institute, for example, has identified more than 2,000 rainforest plants that can help fight cancer cells. In indigenous tribes, a medicine man, or shaman, is traditionally the expert in curing illnesses and ailments.

What cure will plant scientists find next?

## GO-GO GUARANÁ

The Guaraní people of Brazil love the giant guembé plant. They eat its fruits, use the roots to make rope, mash the leaves for insect repellant and treat wounds, burns, snakebites, toothache and conjunctivitis with its sap.

## TRADITIONAL CURES

GUARANÁ - for energy

BALSAM - for colds and coughs

PASSIONFLOWER - to help you sleep

TAYUYA - for pain relief

Annatto seeds are used for a variety of traditional cures - as well as a bright red food dye.

## MODERN DRUGS

* QUININE, from the bark of the cinchona tree - used to treat malaria

* CURARE, from a type of liana - a muscle relaxant/anaesthetic

* VINBLASTINE/VINCRISTINE, from the rosy periwinkle - used in cancer treatment

## KILL OR CURE

Sap from different lianas can be used to cure fevers in children - or to poison and catch fish!

## OTHER USES FOR RAINFOREST PLANTS

Rubber comes from a milky juice called latex in the trunks of certain trees.

The first chewing gum, called chicle, came from the sap of the sapodilla tree.

The sapodilla also produces a sweet, juicy fruit.

# What on Earth is an aye-aye?

LEMURS ARE NAMED AFTER LEMURES – GHOSTS OR SPIRITS FROM ROMAN MYTHS!

Don't you know-know? (Ho ho.) An aye-aye is a type of lemur. If that's no clearer, you might be forgiven, because lemurs live in only one place – Madagascar. Many millions of years ago, this giant island broke away from other land and evolved its own unique wildlife.

Madagascar lies in the Indian Ocean, off the east coast of southern Africa. Around 80 per cent of its plants and animals are endemic, meaning they exist nowhere else on Earth. Madagascar's rainforests are home to loads of unusual creatures, and scientists are finding new ones all the time.

Lemurs are closely related to apes but, separated from the mainland, they evolved differently. There are about 100 different types, from miniature mouse lemurs to the big-bodied indri. Many are critically endangered as people destroy their forest homes.

The nocturnal aye-aye comes to life at night.

Lemurs can communicate using facial expressions!

## LEMUR TROOP

Ring-tailed lemurs live in groups and like to sunbathe together.

## HANDY

Lemurs have fingers and toes like we do. The aye-aye's middle finger is extra long and thin, for digging bugs out of holes that it gnaws in trees!

Many lemurs hang upside down by their feet to eat.

## NOISY

The call of the indri is really loud, like a siren. When one indri calls, others join in with the racket.

## BREAKAWAY ISLANDS

Australia, New Zealand and Papua New Guinea are other islands with many of their own species.

Almost 90% of Australia's reptiles are found nowhere else!

The Australian lizard Boyd's forest dragon won't breathe fire but it will ambush insects.

Look out for carnivorous snails in New Zealand's temperate rainforest. Some have shells as big as a man's fist!

Native to Papua New Guinea, the endangered Huon tree kangaroo is clumsy on land but nifty in the branches.

A tree-climbing kangaroo? Oh yes!

# What's the deadliest rainforest animal?

It's a tough competition. Rainforests are teeming with creatures that could bite, crush or poison a person to death. Of course they're more likely to attack each other! You can make up your own mind out of this lot...

## SAVAGE LEAP

The name jaguar comes from the Native American word yaguar, which means 'he who kills with one leap'. Enough said?

## DEADLY SQUEEZE

As long as a minibus and made of solid muscle - if an anaconda gives you a squeeze, you don't stand much chance. This monster snake can swallow a large animal whole, then not eat again for weeks.

## PEOPLE KILLER

You may be able to squash it with your fingers, but a female Anopheles mosquito can inject you with malaria - one of the world's top killer diseases. Hundreds of thousands of people in the Tropics die every year from a single mozzie bite.

## FLESH-RIPPER

The black caiman is a big, bad cousin of the crocodile. It's the Amazon's largest predator, with flesh-ripping teeth and a ferocious temper.

# POISON!

The Brazilian wandering spider holds the record for most venomous spider in the world. One tiny bite is enough to kill a mouse.

## GIANT

The Goliath bird-eating spider is the biggest spider around. With a leg-span of 28 cm, it's the size of a dinner plate!

A golden poison dart frog has enough poison to kill 10,000 mice – or 10–20 humans. It stores the poison in its skin.

Many poisonous animals are brightly coloured, telling hungry predators to STAY AWAY. If a hunter takes a bite, it will taste revolting and bring on all sorts of ill effects. The unlucky eater won't make the same mistake again!

## SOLDIERS

Army ants march in groups of thousands, killing every insect and small animal in their path.

# Where is the world's stinkiest flower?

We're not talking sweet-smelling roses – some rainforest flowers really WHIFF! The reason they smell so strongly is to attract insects. It's pretty hard to measure a bad smell, but here are some contenders for the pongiest plants on the planet.

NOT SHOWN ACTUAL SIZE

## DEAD MEAT

Another giant that stinks like rancid meat is the titan arum. It can grow up to 3 metres tall and only flowers every 7–10 years.

Rafflesia arnoldi, from Borneo and Sumatra, is also known as the corpse flower. You can probably guess why... it smells of rotting flesh! The stink is all the greater because it's HUGE – the biggest known flower on Earth. It can measure more than a metre across and weigh up to 10 kilograms.

Rafflesias are parasites that live off other plants, using their food and water. They have no leaves, and the flower only blooms for a few days. The pong attracts flies that pollinate the flowers. Rafflesias are either male or female, and the insects have to visit both for the plant to reproduce.

## SLIMY

Bridal veil stinkhorns, a type of fungus, look pretty but ooze a stinky slime.

## TASTY

The smell of the durian has been compared to rotten fish, sewage and over-ripe cheese. But this custardy Southeast Asian fruit tastes great to tigers, sun bears – and people!

Pitcher plants lure insects, mice, birds and even lizards with a tempting sweet scent. Then they trap the prey, squirt it with digestive juices and turn it into a mushy, nutritious soup. **Slurp!**

Some pitcher plants are known as 'monkey cups' because monkeys have been seen drinking rainwater out of them!

Insects slip down here

Filled with insect-digesting fluid

Insects love the brightly coloured flowers of a butterwort. Little do they know, the greasy leaves will trap and slowly suffocate them.

Up to 3 metres across!

## FLOATING GIANT

Victoria amazonica is a giant water lily, with an underwater stalk that's taller than a house. Its leaves can reach 3 metres across – they're fragile but can still hold the weight of a small (and well-behaved) child.

# Why are rainforests shrinking?

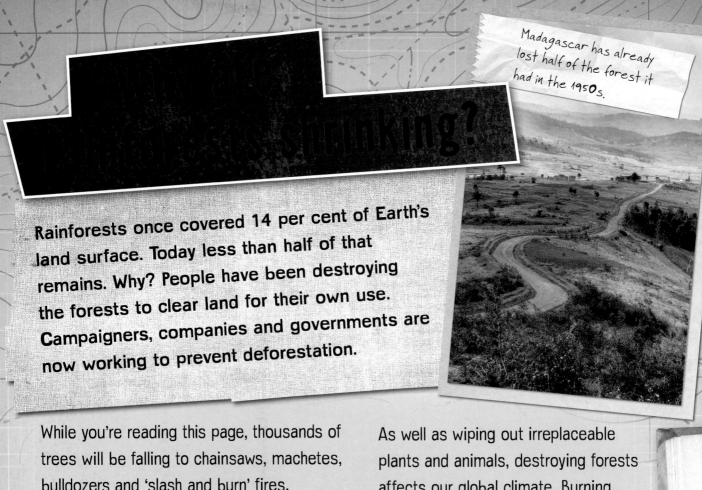

Madagascar has already lost half of the forest it had in the 1950s.

Rainforests once covered 14 per cent of Earth's land surface. Today less than half of that remains. Why? People have been destroying the forests to clear land for their own use. Campaigners, companies and governments are now working to prevent deforestation.

While you're reading this page, thousands of trees will be falling to chainsaws, machetes, bulldozers and 'slash and burn' fires. Mining, logging and agriculture are the main industries to blame. If they continue at the current rate, rainforests could completely vanish in about 40 years.

As well as wiping out irreplaceable plants and animals, destroying forests affects our global climate. Burning trees releases carbon dioxide. Losing forests means less carbon dioxide is soaked up. Tropical deforestation accounts for more than 10 per cent of our greenhouse gas emissions.

A PATCH OF FOREST THE SIZE OF 50 FOOTBALL PITCHES IS CHOPPED DOWN EVERY MINUTE.

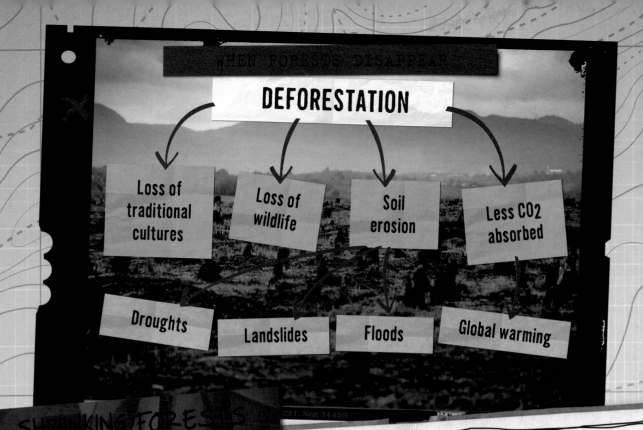

## WHEN FORESTS DISAPPEAR

### DEFORESTATION

- Loss of traditional cultures
- Loss of wildlife
- Soil erosion
- Less CO2 absorbed

- Droughts
- Landslides
- Floods
- Global warming

## SHRINKING FORESTS

### ENDANGERED

Orangutans are close to extinction because their forest homes are being cleared for palm oil plantations.

Over 100 plant and animal species are lost from rainforests every week.

### ACTION

At the 2014 UN Climate Summit, countries pledged to end tropical deforestation by 2030. This could save as many carbon emissions as taking all the world's cars off the roads!

### DEFORESTATION IN BORNEO

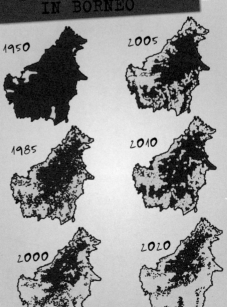

1950

2005

1985

2010

2000

2020

### NATURAL DISASTERS

Plants hold water and protect soil from the drying Sun. Without them, droughts are a threat. Clearing forests can also lead to flooding as plants no longer shield the soil from heavy rains.

### YOU CAN HELP...

Look for sustainable products - food is one of the biggest drivers of deforestation.

Use environmentally friendly paper - better still, recycle and reuse. This book is printed on environmentally friendly paper, so you've already made a start!

Say no to anything containing palm oil.

# What on Earth? words

**altitude** height above sea level

**bromeliad** a type of tropical plant, usually with a short stem and spiny leaves

**camouflage** the ability to blend in with particular surroundings

**canopy** the main treetop layer of a rainforest

**carbon dioxide** a greenhouse gas that plants help to break down

**carnivorous** meat-eating

**cloud forest** a type of tropical rainforest found on hills and mountains and draped in low cloud

**deforestation** clearance of forest by cutting or burning down trees

**drought** a long period of low rainfall

**ecosystem** a community of living things in a particular environment

**ecotourism** controlled tourism in areas of natural beauty that helps to support conservation efforts

**emergents** trees that grow taller than the rainforest canopy level

**endangered** at risk of extinction

**epiphyte** a plant that grows on another plant without feeding off it directly

**Equator** an imaginary line around the Earth, at equal distance from the North and South Poles

**ethnic group** a group of people who share a particular culture, language, etc.

**evolve** to develop gradually over time

**extinction** when a particular species dies out

**germinate** to sprout, or begin to grow from a seed to a plant

**greenhouse gas** a gas in the atmosphere that contributes to global warming

**hunter gatherers** people who live mainly by hunting, fishing and gathering wild food

**indigenous people** the original or native inhabitants of a place

**jungle** another name for a rainforest

**liana** a woody climbing plant, or vine

**malaria** a dangerous tropical disease, spread by the female Anopheles mosquito, which injects a parasite into the blood when it bites

**nocturnal** active at night – nocturnal animals sleep during the day

**nomadic** wandering from place to place rather than having a fixed home

**nutrients** chemicals in food that living things need in order to survive

**palm oil** oil from the fruit of certain palm trees, used in many foods and cosmetics

**parasite** an organism that lives in or on another living thing, using up its nutrients

**photosynthesis** the way green plants use sunlight to convert water and carbon dioxide to food

**pollinate** to transfer powdery pollen from male to female parts of a plant, enabling it to reproduce

**predator** an animal that hunts other animals for food

**sap** fluid that circulates inside a plant

**species** a particular type of plant or animal

**temperate rainforest** a forest found in cooler regions with very high rainfall

**transpiration** the process whereby a plant takes in water and releases water vapour

**Tropic of Cancer/Tropic of Capricorn** imaginary lines around the Earth, north and south of the Equator

**tropical rainforest** a lowland forest with very high rainfall, found in tropical regions close to the Equator

**venomous** injecting a poisonous fluid by biting or stinging

# Further information

## BOOKS

***Trekking in the Congo Rainforest***
*(Travelling Wild)* by Alex Woolf, Wayland, 2014

***What Happens if the Rainforests Disappear?***
*(Unstable Earth)* by Mary Colson, Wayland, 2014

***Rainforests*** *(Research on the Edge)*
by Louise Spilsbury, Wayland, 2014

***Tropical Rainforests*** *(Amazing Habitats)*
by Tim Harris, Franklin Watts, 2015

***Rainforest Animals*** *(Saving Wildlife)*
by Sonya Newland, Franklin Watts, 2014

***Rainforest Rough Guide*** by Paul Mason,
A & C Black, 2011

***Bloomin Rainforests*** *(Horrible Geography)*
by Anita Ganeri and Mike Phillips, Scholastic, 2008

## WEBSITES

http://kids.mongabay.com
Packed with info about rainforests, including the latest environmental news.

http://environment.nationalgeographic.com/
environment/habitats/rainforest-profile/
Discover articles about rainforests and deforestation.

http://www.rainforest-alliance.org/kids/facts
Facts and information from conservationists at the Rainforest Alliance.

http://kids.nceas.ucsb.edu/biomes/
rainforest.html
Find out about life in the rainforest and other world biomes.

http://www.monteverdeinfo.com/
monteverdes-cloud-forests.html
Explore Costa Rica's cloud forest.

http://www.exploringnature.org/db/detail.
php?dbID=44&detID=590
Get to grips with temperate rainforests.

http://www.pbs.org/wnet/africa/explore/
rainforest/rainforest_people_lo.html
Discover Africa's rainforest, its people and their traditions.

## CLIPS

http://www.bbc.co.uk/nature/places/
Amazon_Basin#p003wfcj
Watch rainforest animals get a soaking.

http://www.bbc.co.uk/nature/places/
Amazon_Basin#p0039zg5
Discover wildlife in the amazing Amazon.

http://video.nationalgeographic.com/video/
monkey_spider
See what life is like as an acrobatic spider monkey

https://wwwyoutube.com/watch?v=REPoVfN-
Ij4
Hear howler monkeys howl!

https://wwwyoutube.com/
watch?v=A042J0IDQK4
Watch ants make a raft to float around the flooded forest.

https://wwwyoutube.com/
watch?v=4d3vFI5UpIc
Listen to the singing indri lemur.